Mastering Playwriting
CRAFTING A HIT PLAY
- Natasha Tillett Slayton

Imprint

Book Title: Mastering Playwriting - Crafting a Hit Play
Author: Natasha Tillett Slayton

Author: Natasha Tillett Slayton
Contact: wakdeamay@gmail.com

Mastering Playwriting - Crafting a Hit Play

Written By
Natasha Tillett Slayton

India
2024

CONTENTS

Are you here because you want to write plays? That is great; I applaud your desire. Once we discuss it further in person and you have begun writing plays from our books together, maybe we can discuss if buying this book was indeed the correct choice.

As the title of this book suggests, I assume you want to learn from me how to create a successful play; unfortunately, however, that's something I cannot offer you at this time. Unfortunately for you though, that means I have no clue on how that should work; therefore I raise another question - "What constitutes a successful play?" So feel free to use some black adhesive tape and stick the word "Successful" across the front cover - our collective understanding will determine whether we remove or change this label at some point along this book's journey - let's start looking.
Are You Wondering Why I Wrote This Book on Playwriting? And Why Did I Claim I Could Teach How to Script A Play?? You might be asking why I wrote a book like this on how to script a play, why I believe I can offer assistance?

Well, I have been writing plays for almost 20 years and recently completed my 48th multi-act play. At play premieres I often hear questions from actors regarding writing: "How do you do that? I would also like to write, can't you give some tips on how to?"
So I wrote this book. To tell you how I do it. That was all. Unfortunately, I don't know exactly how many productions of my plays there have been; at one point I gave up trying. But over 1,000 have come together. Because audiences and stages must find my works enjoyable to perform on, that allows me to explain to readers exactly what it takes for me to write plays - writing plays!
If you want to learn how to write plays in an enjoyable and professional manner, or need support while doing it, I would strongly suggest joining working groups or seminars. Adult education courses sometimes provide these as well. One such working group for Low German playwrights - such as Verden's group for Low German playwrights - could be of particular help here - don't be put off by its name "Low German", though. By writing plays using Low German language we strive to preserve it but even if you can't speak or write Low German it won't matter either! Once finished writing plays with this group you could even find translators to translate them into other languages/dialects!
Verden Working Group seminars typically occur twice each year and cover specific topics. Due to newcomers joining, a short basic course is often offered as an introduction to play writing; you can find information online about this option as well

as consider whether or not this might be something worth doing for you. Of course there may still be other paths available.

Other working groups and methods exist for exploring how a play is written.

Your hand does not hold the textbook of an experienced playwright when reading this book; I am just someone who came to writing through theater and has since found themselves prolific writers. All I can offer here are my experiences, advice and tips based on them - nothing else. Please remember this book does not provide rules you must abide by, though; rather I can only describe my approach.

If that was not enough for you and you feel disappointed by this book, then perhaps this book isn't the one for you. Please accept my apology; perhaps exchange or give as a present; I hope that any adhesive strips from the cover sheet can be removed without damaging them as exchange will otherwise become difficult. However, should you wish to learn how Helmut Schmidt writes plays I would welcome that experience as much as any.

Let me start off by saying this about myself: I know for certain that I defy all writing rules! No laws dictate the way a writer must write; however, there are guidelines which need to be adhered to when creating material for publication. Recommending (and I use the word intentionally), writing a play should proceed like this: you already have your plot in your mind (an expression used to define causal connections from an imagined course of events to an expected ending), so creating some form of schedule by hand would be ideal. This means: Once you know your overall storyline, write out exactly what happens in each act and scene until the very end. Once this stage has been reached, writing can begin in earnest on either notebook paper or a computer. Most editors advise playwrights to adopt this approach when writing plays; and most playwrights certainly follow that route when starting to pen their piece(s). That said, I do it differently - only having an idea and starting writing.

My writing process doesn't follow a rigid schedule and expo. Instead, I think about which characters to cast before creating an outline in my head of what could happen, then begin typing the entire play directly into my notebook. Unfortunately, I never know exactly how the piece will progress or end; my plays take shape only through writing them - in many cases all I know at first is its title! So if you like my approach to writing we may make great partners!

Oh - one more thing: when it comes to writing for theater groups, my focus tends to be amateur productions rather than professional stages - something editors frequently remind me. So there you are. Writing exclusively for professional stages gives me the ability to be more flexible in some respects; I could incorporate multiple sets and costumes. But, what would be the point in offering my work to only a select few theatres who are uninterested? It may take years, perhaps never being performed on amateur stages because the effort it would require would surely exceed their capacities. Doesn't it make more sense to write pieces that can easily and playful implemented by amateur actors while still meeting professional stage quality and level requirements? I believe so and that is why when writing I consider lay groups primarily. Every group needs a play each year. Let's celebrate some classics together that I particularly admire; these will undoubtedly remain popular favorites of mine for many years to come! "My Husband Goes to Sea" and "The Furnished Gentleman" are great classics of theater; however, modern plays (such as "My Husband Goes to Sea" or "The Furnished Gentleman") may have greater relevance. And for theater groups performing their plays in Low German it's particularly crucial that they reach young audiences; that may not happen with works set during the 50s to 70s.

Now is an opportune moment for me to introduce the history of theater and begin by outlining its core characteristics as stated by Aristotle: drama's main characteristic being dialogue-driven action presentation, differentiating it from narrative epic. There could be entire books written on this topic but instead I suggest listening in on seminars or visiting online sources in order to discover its roots.

Are you still open to collaboration? I welcome it. Let's walk together along this road leading towards producing our first play, which might even become successful! I look forward to helping. I am happy.

About 25 kilometers from my parents' house I worked as a disc jockey at a discotheque on weekends from 1984 - 1991, one of those small village discos which no longer exist today. There I played single records by C.C. Richards as well as songs written specifically for this disco by other composers such as Johnny Stein (which sadly no longer exist today). Catch, Modern Talking as well as U2 and Queen were playing from the speakers that night, as I served as one of the DJs responsible for providing information to guests through my microphone about each artist or song as we played each track and get them excited! Dancing was great fun; anyone who dances a lot needs something to drink; clever business tactic! Every evening I was allowed to fulfill musical requests of young ladies like Edeltraud Trey who always wanted "Touch by Touch" by Joy as her chosen tune. This is where Edeltraud Trey came into my life! At one point Edeltraud told me she was participating in theater with an amateur group and that their premiere was coming up soon. I attended and really enjoyed their performance; almost one year later Edeltraud told me one of their members had left and they desperately wanted to reunite as soon as possible.

As Edeltraud wanted someone "younger", I decided to join Stapelmoor theater group in Rheiderland and play Edeltraud's young lover - always playing my part well and thoroughly enjoying theater performance! After my second year, however, I noticed that many of the pieces selected by Spolbaas weren't very modern and started exploring other theater groups and what works they were performing. Between 20 theater groups operating around Leer, many performed traditional or even classic 1950s-style plays. At that time, my friends and I would play in Low German; at that time it was already becoming clear that this language must be promoted more in kindergartens and schools because more and more children were only hearing Standard German from their parents. As I considered how best to promote Low German in amateur theater groups, it dawned on me that simply performing old pieces from the 50s and 60s wouldn't work. Theater should also exist today if it is to remain relevant. Attracting young people to theater and Low German was of particular concern. I rehearsed "Funfair in 't Dorp" with my theater group in 1989 - featuring several amusing moments but otherwise being just another farmer's comedy from the 60s. In the summer of the same year, I started using an Olympia typewriter and attempted to write my own play. While at that time I only had minimal gaming experience, my goal was to write something about an approaching silver wedding anniversary as my first work. She wants a big celebration - he has been unemployed for several weeks but leaves the house every morning, hiding his fate from his wife so as not to ruin her joy at this exciting milestone. My plot revolved around finding ways of paying for this celebration; hence the creation of three-act play "Two Boys Too Many". In late summer 1989 my work was completed despite initially feeling embarrassed; thanks to Edeltraud's support it has since been performed numerous times with great success.

Diedrich Wessels was our game director. He said it was too long and needed to be reduced down significantly; I worked on that with him and we premiered it with our theater group in Stapelmoor in February 1990 - almost always playing to sold-out audiences? Do you consider that to be a successful play?

How has 2018 differed from prior years? I don't believe so; it is an entirely normal response when people learn of an amateur theater group member writing their first work and people become curious to see it - this doesn't reflect success but has good reviews nonetheless. As I wrote the comedy with laughter in mind, but without being too "flat," inquiries came quickly from various stages who wanted to know where this piece could be seen; thus forcing me to find publishers. As I knew our theater group purchased plays from Karl Mahnke in Verden - still Germany's leading publisher when it comes to Low German plays and where many well-known classics are published - I submitted my work and hoped that it would be accepted there. But after some weeks had gone by, my manuscript was returned and I was informed it could not be published as is and needed work done on it before publication could occur. Additionally, I was invited to visit the Verden working group which left me indignant; having played the lead role in an incredible play several weeks prior which received standing ovations, it made no sense why these same people are writing me letters saying my work wasn't good enough when they hadn't even seen it themselves!

Today I can laugh about it; but take my word for it - the same can happen to you. After my initial work had been accepted for publication, I became part of Dieter Jorschick's working group - I don't regret being taught there as what was taught had an enormous influence on the quality and level of my subsequent works, with which we often disagreed (sometimes very strongly!) As one who wasn't easily intimidated, I did not want to wait after finishing my piece to edit or change anything either - instead I was impetuous about making decisions and wanted my work published immediately after first work had been finished - something Dieter Jorschick made possible with his patience while sometimes disagreeable (though). Defiant as ever, when it came time to edit or alter anything at all (even a significant impactful effect in improving later works that we discussed during working group.) Dieter Jorschick taught us invaluable in these matters! (although we often disagreed!) Although sometimes stubborn and stubborn myself to edit afterwards! But after finishing it was decidedly published immediately with no changes needed after having written something new so quickly after starting something so quickly; that meant having read through again before beginning editing process of course (never mind...).

As inquiries from various groups had already come in, what should I do? I searched for another publisher and recorded my essay there; although, slightly edited for them as well. Once that was done, my confidence increased rapidly; thus leading me to start the next piece immediately; which eventually lead me onto writing more and more of them! Suddenly, I became an extremely prolific writer - yes - some editors think otherwise but not for me; my work doesn't need intensive revision when you are producing more work! I think otherwise!

Well, everything happened back in 1990 and now I've just performed my 48th multi-act play under this title: Four hands for one udder". - As its script.

Time slips away...

But let me first take care in asking why it is that you want to write a play. Putting aside any talk of success at this point - we don't know each other and nothing about your background would suggest that it would suit as an author - don't panic; writing doesn't require a doctorate, specific training or diploma, which I certainly didn't possess myself (so we both start from square one!). So who could it be you are trying to be? Here are a few examples:

Are you male in his early 40s, working as a real estate agent, married, with three children, playing senior men's team football in your free time and have recently been persuaded by your wife to join an amateur theater group she has been involved with for years, which you really enjoy and that now excites and thrills you so much that writing plays has become something you want to try yourself? - All right then.

Imagine this: you are a single woman in her late 50s or early retiree years who is experiencing some boredom at home but enjoys going to theater events occasionally and thinking: surely I can do what this author wrote down? - Accepted.

Your early 20s is full of uncertainty about which career path to take. Are you an avid reader with strengths in German and essay writing from school? - Excellent. Are you passionate about theater? - Fantastic.

Do any of the examples resonate with you? No matter your age, type of training or reason for wanting to write, what's key is that your writing comes from within - whether that is engaging with theater and its topic. And above all: you must set aside enough time for this work as a playwright - I started as part-time job and continue this practice today - this approach is absolutely fine, just be sure you make use of every waking hour available to write!

At its core, writing should be fun for you - reading is even better - as is going to the theater. By having been onstage before - even on an amateur stage - and performing some roles yourself - you are much better prepared for becoming an author yourself - something I myself did when beginning this endeavor.

Although I do not know your motivations for wanting to write, it could be that a play has annoyed you and you want to change it? Perhaps you watched a performance, perhaps on an established stage, where it failed to entertain? Or have audience members in your theater group noticed better productions from previous years; or even you were dissatisfied with both its overall piece and your role. So you want to improve it? Why not? -

Are you writing a play because it would be fun and would bring in additional income as part of your full-time job? - That is great too. Whatever the motivation may be - all that really matters is that it fulfills a deep-seated need within you to write something dramatic! The main thing is simply doing what makes sense for YOU - no matter the motivations behind why.

Are You Still There and Are You Ready? (O.k.). That said, let us continue. Many believe writing is something inherited; people with writing abilities don't learn it through academic studies alone - there must be something genetic about their talent that comes through; someone needs an inclination for something like this in them." [Such people] tend to think "Oh if someone can write, it must have come from somewhere deep within themselves - you can't learn it unless there's already talent there]. But that doesn't need be true; everyone can learn it if given enough support. [Such people often believe] [...] but learning is possible!" Its People tend to think:

At age 10 in 5th grade, my mother would often write my essays for school that I was having difficulty with - the usual ones like: "My Most Beautiful Holiday Experience" or "The Thunderstorm", as dictated by teachers. These types of narrative essays were difficult for me; my mother excelled at this; in 20 minutes she completed beautiful essays for me that consistently earned good grades at school - thank you Mama! Unfortunately my interest in writing only emerged later on as an adult of 25.

No law exists that sets forth specific requirements for becoming a playwright. As long as you meet some or all of the following criteria, however, your career as a playwright should go smoothly:

Are you someone who enjoys socializing, both talking to others and listening?

Do you like staying informed on world and local events, reading newspapers and novels alike, attending theater, cinema, opera and concerts as well as cultural events such as lectures?

Are you someone who enjoys watching films on television, as well as various talk shows, reports and series from time to time? Can you predict halfway through how a film will end?

Can you answer yes to any or all of these points? Well then what are we waiting for?

Of course, you could buy a pad and pencil and start writing, but no publisher today will accept a handwritten manuscript as submission material. Writing may no longer be possible in our modern age without computers, storage media and word processing programs such as Word. I would strongly advise using "Word" for playwriting projects that will be published. Text Capture and Editing Software by Microsoft; Publishers also often rely on it. For optimal performance, specialist retailers offer the latest version. Though this program costs approximately 100 euros to purchase, its benefits don't stop with simply entering text on a computer; notebook users also benefit. Years of working exclusively on notebooks has given me the advantage of flexibility; I can take them with me anywhere and use the device whenever necessary. Both hardware (the notebook) and software (Word) are now ready and waiting to capture any ideas that arise. If this process is too quick for your liking and you prefer working without computers, if this approach seems too fast-paced then starting out using pad and pencil may also work; going forward you may always carry around a small booklet and pen in order to take notes as necessary; but your final work must go into a computer; therefore it would be wiser for you to get used to using one from day one.

Start by finding the ideal space in which to write. Certain authors insist it must be an empty room with your desk in its place - simply close the door behind you, put aside everything around you and begin writing with total focus!
Well, if that is how some authors write, there's nothing wrong with that; but to suggest writing can only occur this way is complete nonsense.
Find a space that speaks to you, and don't allow anyone else to dictate where or how it should look. I think having plenty of lighting and an inviting ambience are especially essential. I certainly have an office with a desk; however, I also enjoy writing in my living room while lying on the sofa with the notebook resting against my thighs and waiting for inspiration to strike. No need for absolute silence either; beautiful music helps my focus! Chris de Burgh's writing style is one that I particularly appreciate for writing outside in nice weather - I enjoy sitting outside on the terrace or park bench and writing while taking long train journeys, too! Even on flights I often write. There are even authors who enjoy sitting at cafes with their notebook and writing in front of other people; if this approach speaks to you - explore it! Everything is possible.

As far as writing goes, the location is entirely up to you; find somewhere comfortable where you feel most relaxed but make sure that other people do not interrupt or

disturb too often; this should enable you to concentrate. If you have family, just inform them beforehand that you would like some uninterrupted time for writing.
Time of Day to Write
As soon as you feel ready and motivated to write, take the plunge! When your mood has soured or you feel downhearted - perhaps because someone important has passed on - don't write. Wait a day or two until your spirits improve before starting writing again. If something has upset you deeply - such as losing one of your closest friends - writing can often bring comfort.
If a loved one has died or you are experiencing something more significant that's bothersome to you, writing is likely impossible - this process may even take weeks or months! Don't even bother trying!

Do not force yourself to write just for the sake of distracting from any bad mood, since this doesn't work. Let alone thinking about it as such an option!
No set rules exist regarding how long writers should write for, but one to two hours at a time (that's roughly 1000 words) should suffice for productive work. Avoid only writing once every month as then it will become very hard to find your thread again - instead live your work. Think about and discuss with others your piece when not typing; some ideas for its further development often arise even without typing anything! Be aware of what has already been written so far and anticipate what may happen next (scene, act). Feel free to take breaks - even for several days - whenever it suits! You are welcome even when taking breaks - feel free even for days on end!
Playwrights have once shared with me that it takes two years for them to write a play - typically writing 20 pages before placing it away for three months and returning three months later to further work on it. When finally finished in its rough version form after several months have passed, then they rework it once more and over.
Imagine my surprise to learn of this news; such an arrangement would never cross my mind! However, if writing remains our joint passion then forget this matter as life moves swiftly by.
Have we discussed everything so far, then? Wonderful. - So let's get down to work now that everything is ready? Are your computer or notebook equipped, or at least a pad and pen, as well as an ideal work space ready? Now is an opportune time and place for us all. Let's go for it - that should do it for now.
Preparations is complete, and now it is time to focus on the main issue - your first stage play!

Your play begins with its basic idea. Typically this can be described in one long sentence that poses questions rather than statements; from here the characters and plot usually form organically - for instance:
"Imagine this: If a gynecologist diagnosed a 45-year-old as pregnant; but on the same day her daughter attended with the same last name for a blood sample collection and something went awry, what would the outcome be?" (the recipe for success)
How will one of Germany's richest families react when news reports suggest a comet will hit earth within weeks and probably end all life on Earth? *(Pyramids of Time) Musical currently in development
"What would happen if two unemployed men began offering an escort service for women?"*(Welcome to Chez Andre) "Two homeless individuals had been using an abandoned holiday home on an island for shelter during winter months, yet this house is being sold and a family is moving in"*(Heideweg No. 11)
An amateur chemist creates a serum intended to eliminate all trace of sweat odor, and will conduct tests with voluntary test subjects." *(The crazy professor).
*Titles of my pieces that were inspired by these basic ideas. mes Did you understand it? Just one sentence usually suffices for an idea; writing down one can even help. Ideas can come to us anywhere and anytime; for instance, in 1991 when Renate and Stefan Brommelhaup got married at our work facility, they told me about all their intensive wedding preparations months in advance - I attended their ceremony as an observer sitting in church and watching.

Do you know the answer to that question? In the play, everything that could possibly go wrong during wedding preparations and the actual ceremony does! This makes for great comedy that audiences love!
I think that's part of why this piece is performed so frequently; most audiences have witnessed at least one wedding in their family; or their own, before watching this play. Making your most beautiful day (sometimes not!!) memorable requires thorough preparation - even then things might still go wrong, which makes for even greater drama when seen onstage! And because nobody wants to experience it first-hand, audiences appreciate seeing such portrayals play out before them onstage!
Let me provide another example of how dramaturgy works. If your writing lacks moments that become riveting or suspenseful after several pages, then your piece does not qualify as dramatic - the play cannot function without conflict and tension!
Build Banality! This is an excellent way to learn drama. This two-stage process works perfectly! Pay Attention!

A young lady at a fair is looking at an empty Ferris wheel which rotates slowly around it.

Do you find this topic and its drama intriguing and riveting? Perhaps not; in that case, what questions come to your mind as soon as you imagine this scene?

Can anyone explain why the woman in this picture is alone at the fair? Are they thinking about riding the Ferris wheel and enjoying its ride? My questions have almost run their course... I don't even want to know more, since looking at an empty Ferris wheel at a fair can be very boring - or do they even need any answers?!?!?

So now let's extend that sentence:

A young lady at a fair is watching a full and rotating ferris wheel when suddenly someone falls 30 meters from one of its gondolas! Wow! Now THAT is dramatic!

And then come the questions: Why did that person fall from the gondola? Was it an accident or murder? Who were in this gondola, including who the young woman is who is sitting with.... Do you want another example to help familiarise yourself with dramatic moments? - Yes, please!

Young, happy couples want to get married. Both want to do it "virginally".

Well, that may seem unconventional these days - but that's up to each individual to decide. What queries or inquiries arise from this sentence? Perhaps one: why both individuals wish to delay until their wedding? We extend this thought:

Shortly before their wedding date, an unhappy, young couple decide to enter marriage without knowing they are pregnant - only for it to turn out that shortly thereafter the young woman is pregnant! Needless to say, now there are more questions than answers for everyone involved.

Please give it a try to create dramaturgy or an exciting point through sentences such as this - it really works! Additionally, your ideas might make their way into your piece! Do you already have an idea what your first piece should be about?

This principle should help determine whether you want to write a comedy, crime novel, play or musical. Also keep in mind whether or not you wish to choose between sketch writing, one act plays and multi act plays and which language(s) to write in.

Back then, I immediately began with a multi-act play and have focused solely on comedies ever since. For this book's purposes, we will discuss full-length comedies. As standard German is my recommended language of choice (though Low German may work if translated or has it done to High German by publishing your piece, publisher usually also receive rights to translate your play or novel into other dialects such as Dutch, Swiss German or other). As Low German may not be something all people can speak fluently just yet we will write our piece using standard German instead -

though Low German may work if writing first draft is needed in Low German as Low German can translate into High German before being translated again before being translated again before writing it all in High German instead unless we decide upon writing our piece!

Your initial idea for the play should not come from anywhere. Do not make the mistake of writing about someone going to prison for tax evasion and telling his relatives they're joining the military again, only for their ship to sink later on - nor write about a theater group that stages plays with dress rehearsal and premiere scenes taking place within one act, with humorous results.

Theater enthusiasts already recognize these concepts: my husband goes to sea" and "Nothing but mess". If you write something similar to these, it can cause problems with other authors claiming rights to it; therefore it would be best to create your own idea for a piece and find your own audience for it instead of plagiarizing something that already exists. With thousands of stage plays already out there already written, are these still possible today? What topic or ideas could spark something fresh in 2008 and beyond?

What idea has yet to be utilized fully?

No one would accuse you of being completely mistaken if you believe that all basic themes have already been explored. These might include inheritance, winning the lottery, birth of a child, unemployment or bankruptcy and more.

All these elements exist already, yet with just the right combination, something new emerges - an incomparable piece. That is precisely what it's up to you to achieve.

Have an open mind and use your imagination when looking for inspiration; even if your plot comes from another source like film or novel it should only be taken as inspiration and not copied directly in dialogue form for publication as your play. Indulge your creative side and try coming up with something yourself.

Now let's come up with an idea for your first piece. What do you make of this: "A 70-year-old woman still operating a corner shop should be deported by her children to a retirement home." What associations or questions spring immediately to mind in response? Close the book first and think deeply about this statement before writing down what comes to mind, then read further down this idea to see if any similar questions arise for yourself - I quickly thought up five such queries myself!

Why are the children trying to deport their mother?

What will become of the store and what are its children planning to do with it?
How is mother behaving - plans she is making with others etc?

And finally how is nursing home paid for?

Did my thoughts match yours? - Did you find the topic engaging? I hope so - this idea is mine, yet no play has been written about it by any author as yet.

There isn't much confusion regarding what this topic encompasses. Sure, there are plays with nursing and retirement homes as a theme; one was performed at Ohnsorg Theater in Hamburg just last summer under the title "Atschuss mien Leeve", while classics also feature them prominently; but we create our own work using nursing homes as backdrop rather than as stage sets.

As our first step in developing our piece, the first thing we should do is identify when it should take place. You have complete freedom here - choose any time period from now until the 1970s (amateur theaters may find this more challenging), although costume, stage design, language and currency all must match accordingly if playing an amateur theater piece from this period - such as costumes and stage design from those decades - will require extra care when performing. Amateur theaters tend to struggle more with this than professional stages when doing the piece itself but some still do this by moving it forward 20-30 years - something which would never happen in an amateur theatre production! So we agreed on starting from 2008 for our joint work - is that okay with you? Unfortunately I cannot offer much else since most of my pieces take place between then and now as my pieces generally don't exist within that era either!

I think it would be possible to present this work again without making significant modifications, starting in 2008 due to Germany's slow pace of change. Even by 2015 it should still be relevant and could still happen - don't take my word for it; just be assured it could happen as planned. World is constantly shifting; technology in particular is an incredible force of evolution that sometimes worries me; if I buy a cell phone today, it will likely become obsolete by tomorrow if not sooner! With plays, however, it is common to expect them to remain playable for 10-20 years without modification - something I observed with works I wrote 10 years ago that have survived almost unchanged despite our currency shifting from Deutsche Mark (DM) to Euro. Your piece can therefore continue being enjoyed by audiences for quite some time!

Who knows; perhaps in 50 years this film will become a timeless classic!

We should now address stage design. Over the years I have met numerous amateur theater groups who put forth great effort into their stage designs; some even view it as an opportunity to show audiences something special. But few groups voluntarily choose complex stage sets. Furthermore, many people avoid showing multiple stage sets; for some groups this is even impossible; perhaps at some point when writing plays it will become necessary to show all of the action using only one set. I've experienced it first-hand and found it quite harmless; some amateur theaters actually do this well. Although professional ensembles may use revolving stages without issue, our focus should remain amateur stages; which amateur theater has one already? If you want your piece to be read widely and performed often, avoid elaborate sets with multiple components. Theater groups have the flexibility of changing stage sets quickly while completely different images may put them off - even if your piece is appreciated by theater groups.

Now you may be asking what sort of stage set to use. Your options for creating this are vast - heaven or hell are two good starting points; for the latter option request and describe this stage setting accordingly. Consider taking on locations like restaurants, bakeries, gardens, churches, campsites or terraces as possible settings; alternatively wait rooms, brothels, clubhouses, hospital rooms and construction sites are also suitable options...
As we all know from classic films like "Gossip in the Stairwell" and "The Furnished Gentleman", hallways can make excellent settings. When writing your story and wanting your characters to take place somewhere specific - like space or the moon - any set will do. Remember that all actors must be visible within this stage set!
As this is where most characters congregate, authors usually select living rooms or kitchen-cum-living rooms as stage settings for their stories. This makes sense since living rooms and kitchen-cum-living rooms are the focal points of apartments; thus making their use as stage sets natural and realistic. Toilets in single family homes would seem even more inappropriate as stage settings; no wonder it hasn't caught on any further! - However, nothing stands against using large toilets with several cubicles and sinks (e.g. hotel or restaurant bathrooms) as stage sets; I've never seen one before but if this would bothers you then please don't hesitate - I don't mind at all if that would bothers you then please let me know!

Are You Fascinated by Different Stage Designs? - Are You interested in an extraordinary stage design, or even different ones for each act of your piece? All right.

So maybe a brothel for Act I of your work, then construction site Act II and space Act III... I advise against it but encourage experimenting as this would require professional stage builders who could achieve what you ask - something amateur groups are less capable of doing compared to professional builders - with each act having three unique sets requiring separate building crews - hence what would it bring you out? - And more than likely results would come out from it... so what can amateur groups get out of multiple stage set designs than trying something like this...? - Amateurs shy away from complex sets like this!

Now we need to agree on a stage design for your first work, but which should we select? One option would be for us to focus on a woman, her children and this small shop as our setting. Given that she will likely play one of the main roles, ideally this setting should take place where this person often spends her time such as where your shop may be set as this could serve as the perfect stage set - however please keep the following factors in mind before doing this:

Displaying a fully furnished store requires considerable work for groups; there will likely be food and props needed. Should the woman need to enter retirement home (we don't yet know whether her children can manage that or not), what will become of the store afterwards. Depending on developments, likely it would open again as another venture.

Stage design takes time and effort, so I suggest setting this piece in this woman's kitchen-living room, with an indirect passageway leading directly to a shop in the background. This looks really nice and allows viewers to imagine it even though they won't see it directly. Sorry we're returning to eating-in kitchens; but this solution seems ideal here. Do you agree? Excellent.

At the outset of any play, its author must describe its stage design. Not only must you keep in mind the stage set design but also rooms not visible to audience but still significant for what is occurring; though you do not need to describe these. Every stage setting needs an entrance and exit - in this instance a door. Where it is placed will depend on your piece - if it doesn't matter, simply write that in your description. Imagine our stage design such that the large passageway leading to the shop is placed towards the back - against its back wall - so as to face away from any possible distractions from outside. On its right is a door leading directly outside; while on its left is another one that leads into other rooms. Kitchen, Bedroom and Bathroom) As our protagonist won't always be present in either the shop, kitchen or out of the house; therefore the left door makes perfect sense as an entryway into other parts of our protagonist's residence. So if we now have three doors (or two doors and a passage), it is necessary to determine whether a window is still needed or desirable. A window always adds visual interest; but if its purpose for your piece has no significance (noone needs to look in or out, no escape through window etc), simply do without or leave it to stage design.

Based on your size and possibilities, stage design may be handled in-house by yourself. If the writing or creative process gives rise to an idea for something playful with windows or their frames that is also integral to stage design, this is necessary; but do not force theater company's set designers with details that do not contribute anything substantial or necessary for play; simply because it makes for more creative writing! Consider that idea in your head. My suggestion does not require windows; two doors (right and left) with passage leading back into the shop are sufficient.

Now that we know our goals are clear, let's set up the room. Please provide as much detail as possible but leave enough wiggle room for groups to create their own artwork; and try not to include details that are unnecessary for the piece. As a game director and stage builder, if you describe an ash gray couch as being prominent in a room, I would want to know why that particular color matters so much to your piece. So leave something like this out just because that's how you envision it, even though it has absolutely no relevance. As soon as your play is published and performed, you are sure to witness several productions of it - each production differing considerably in stage design elements as well. Before making requests, be sure to consider those components which support and strengthen your piece as part of its stage design needs. Furniture should match each character. Since we have decided on an older lady for our play (let's call her Lady X for now), I assume that she will be one of the likeable characters within it. At 70, she may not be doing especially well financially - yet may still wish to run the corner shop as a source of enjoyment. But if she's well liked in her workplace, then her money management will certainly be better managed - something which also impacts on our stage design - that could certainly alter its appearance differently in an unsympathetic wealthy person's living room versus that of Lady X? - Right now I see a clean and cozy kitchen-living room that neither indicates wealth nor poverty. Are you the same way? However, if we imagine that Queen X's children take all her earnings away, forcing her to run the store even in her old age despite its financial strain - then the situation changes entirely and stage design can certainly become more sparse.
Right from the opening of the stage, our lady's poverty becomes obvious through stage design - without needing any dialogue - making an immediate statement without needing dialogue from any of our actors. Unfortunately, this turns into more of a drama because the topic seems very serious and dramatic... I thought we had agreed

on comedy- and this second option for stage design was not quite what we agreed upon - I hope that you feel similarly.

Imagine this room furnished and describe it in your piece. Kitchen-living rooms typically contain seating, such as a corner bench or simply table and chairs; given our lady is already 70, an armchair may make more sense; BUT: Don't hesitate to play around and use props and furniture creatively!

If there's a Chinese sculpture in your piece, its presence should make sense in terms of context. If a CD player or television are listed among your description criteria then these should make a reasonable contribution as well.

At some point in a scene builder's efforts will require using devices for ballast and effort. When this comes up in an acting scene, write it down that this photo belongs to it if one appears. If an actor uses one in an action scene on an adjacent wall then note it down too! If this framed photograph should come to be part of another scene then write that location down too as evidence that this particular photo comes from it.

Starting off, pictures should be hung as part of your game from the very start. If an image isn't part of the game, however, don't feel limited by having it hanging directly on a wall; nice little objects you might find around your kitchen could work just as well; most stage builders tend to incorporate such decorations anyway.

Stage Design (Calendars, Flowers, Decoration of Table and Cabinets etc) Have I made myself clear? No? Allow me to illustrate what the stage design for this piece might entail:

Stage Design:

This stage design depicts Mrs.... (Lady X's) kitchen-living room. At the back, an opening leads into their grocery store - visible from all seats - featuring various food packages and beverages available there, advertising signs for said store as well as advertising signs promoting said grocery store. A curtain made of wooden beads or plush strips prevents anyone from seeing through to it unless someone walks through. There is one door leading outside onto both right and left sides.

Lady X's living space is comfortably and simply furnished, featuring a sofa, two armchairs (or corner bench), table, cupboard and telephone; there are also phone jacks and CD players nearby as well as three photographs on the walls depicting her deceased husband, their Son and herself (see figure on right).

Daughter-in-law and grandchild) with some novels on display on an open shelf attached to a wall.

If you need multiple sets for other plays you are writing, detail each individual scene individually: Act 1:- Act 2:etc. Satisfied? - Okay, when I was thinking through our stage design I realized I would use the telephone at some point; music could also add depth. For Lady X to read; pictures on your walls symbolize family warmth that could also have meaning in this piece; here I have already thought through our characters who will feature in future chapters of our play!

Many authors, myself included, like to use the following popular sentence at the end of stage descriptions: "All other equipment is left up to the playgroup". This allows set designers some freedom while at the same time expecting theater groups to put things on stage that seem appropriate based on play and dialogue. Most amateur theater groups put great care and thought into their designs; unfortunately not every person manages this feat!

What we learned now was simply outlining the set requirements for this piece.

However, the same principles apply for every stage design you need: describe it in great detail while still leaving some free space on stage. Once stage sets start going up and taking shape in front of you, your heart may swell; only to later see something amiss when looking back through pictures taken from these sets; this happens all too frequently!

Amateur theater groups - no matter how thoroughly you outline their stage design - sometimes forget some essential pieces, even after taking steps to include everything necessary for success in their stage design. When it comes to props that only need to be used once per act, such as those needed before each scene at the start of each act. Occasionally this means missing them altogether! When that occurs they should not be included as part of the overall set, but before each scene.

At this point, stage design should be complete. You have gained enough understanding about what stage sets can and should be requested from various groups as a stage set, and what should be avoided altogether.

Assuming we already have an idea and stage set described, let's move onto one of the most crucial chapters: characters or protagonists. One key decision will be how many to include; should I include just my ideal number, or should I also consider my capacity and consider other elements that come into play as part of their decision process? Fact: Your piece can include 20 or more actors without breaking any rules; performances staged and shown at open-air theaters often feature 30-50 actors at once, especially historical productions which usually use even more. I love watching things like that. There's also plenty of space outside; a large open-air stage could easily accommodate 50 performers if necessary, but for our purposes here, let's focus on small spaces or stages which could also feature large performers. Amateur theater groups usually only require a certain number of active actors; the number depends entirely on your ideas and plotline - sometimes twelve may suffice; other times only four are necessary. At premieres of my plays, directors often request more players. Our group consists of 15 active members; it would be wonderful if all 15 could participate." Meanwhile, when in another city I often hear: "Oh please write more pieces with less players in future; our group only comprises 6 individuals and not everyone wants a role".

"Well, as it is hard to please every stage, here is my recommendation: For 7 to 8 people per piece to ensure ease and accessibility on most stages. However, you could try writing one with 6, 10 or 13 people as an alternative; but generally speaking 7-8 is optimal."

Every character requires a name. You can give each of them their own distinctive identity; however, avoid using names of well-known personalities, as it would seem silly for your protagonists to bear names such as Helmut Kohl, Heidi Kabel or Veronica Ferres - this could even cause conflicts. But even if the names of your characters aren't "famous", please ensure they are the appropriate ones. If there is a prominent company such as Apple that might appear, for example. If A. is run by Hans and Beate Hansen, Ludger Memmen or Detlef Meyer as married partners, then it would be prudent not to mention them directly in your piece. There are people who have little interest in theater, yet hearing or reading their name within an unfamiliar work could cause emotional harm to their personality. If this unfortunate coincidence involves two real people from a large company or similar context; no one should blame you!

My characters often take their names from an old phone book. Now there's also CD-ROM options. When creating my stories I sometimes mix first and last names in creative ways; you decide how best to approach this challenge.

Let's talk about naming our characters and cast for our play. Starting off, Queen X plays an important part. What name would be best suited for her? - Perhaps Leni Kramer from her original name Helene would suffice, or how about Gerda Krupp or Johanna Muchal or Gesine Peters might suit better depending on your personal taste? Another consideration when selecting an appropriate name is considering their ages - for instance Queen X should be around 17-18.

At least 70 years ago, no one would have given birth. Another example: If your play involves a pastor, their children might have names like Simon, John, Mary or Esther - these subtleties can be learned quickly - trust me! Sometimes a name can help define who a character is; that might depend on personal preference; for a likeable young woman I prefer Silvia, Helga or Heidi as names to consider. I tend to associate names such as Katharina, Elisabeth or Gertrud with conflict-prone characters on stage, so when reading their names I tend to envision these women as those responsible. Instead I prefer calling any male figures that seem somewhat awkward Joachim Focko Gerd Heinrich or Kunibert. Sven, Jorg, Andre or Sebastian don't seem like the appropriate names for such characters; don't you agree? But as with anything, this could just be personal opinion. *If any readers identify as Elisabeth or Gertrud and believe themselves to be lovely people then please forgive my comment as an insulting generalization.

By the way, I assume our lady X is of German heritage - hence her German name Helene Kramer (known by Leni).

Who else should star in our play? Leni's son and daughter-in-law? That was on my mind when describing the stage design (photos on walls). If that came back to you - good. Given Leni was married previously, their surnames would likely change; perhaps Rudolf and Ina Pleiss? Why would we? Given our agreement that Leni was widowed, this seems quite appropriate to the story. So far we have three figures; Leni, her son and his wife. If Leni married when she was between 20-30, that gives us 40-50 year-old versions of each. Do they both have children? Would it be acceptable if we took on the role of finding and hiring an individual who has an outstanding relationship with his/her grandmother and could play an integral part in our group entanglements? Would Daniel Pleiss work? Fine. With such an age range there would always be room for growth among groups - for everyone involved.

Characters in the piece. Please only request specific age information if it is truly necessary; for instance, I could give an example such as: "The 75th Birthday". Ideally, though, an actor would first portray themselves as being aged 74-years-old before portraying that character onstage. Our piece centers on Leni's realization of retirement age, and this will likely come up in her dialogue. Therefore, his age should reflect reality more accurately than other characters'. So for our Leni, that number stands at 70! Theater groups now need to present an actress aged 70 years for this role, yet make-up artists are able to turn 20-year-olds into old women through make-up artistry. Making someone younger requires more effort; if discussing an exact age becomes relevant in dialogue or is asked outright for it's importance then be sure to state this fact accurately in dialogue or other forms of discussion.

Now to our figures. Now we have four: Leni, Rudolf, Ina and Daniel - do you remember our basic idea? Imagine this scene again with Leni at her store and what might happen. Conflict exists already within our basic idea - in case it slipped your mind... here's a reminder: A 70-year-old woman running a corner shop should be sent away to an assisted retirement facility by her children."

At its core, this story can be divided into "good guys" and "bad guys." That is a good thing as otherwise there would be no conflict - which would render any play mundane and dull. We still require characters who support Leni's side (e.g. her mother or dad). Characters for Leni to discuss her situation with are important: Who could she turn to, friends of similar age with whom she can discuss plans for her children's future, maybe one being widowed as well... Hhm... This could prove quite interesting! Let's choose two: Helga Willms and Trude Lehmann are just two names I came up with - now we already have six figures; are these enough? Personally I would prefer two additional ones just for added complexity - let me know your thoughts below in comments section below! I think so
Your son introduced Leni to an individual whom could potentially become close, becoming serious in love with Leni or just acting as an intermediary in his plotting against Leni? Additionally, how about young women as possible suitors? - Daniel could meet this young lady through either friendship or romantic interest; but what if Leni's son Daniel also had a young lover? Anything is possible and I plan to create both characters; let's call the gentleman Karl-Heinz Ahrens and the young lady Gabi Meyer! At this point, I believe we have completed our list of characters. While additional individuals might be needed, or existing characters eliminated; that will depend on how the piece evolves. Let's put together our complete list, which should appear on page 4 of your manuscript and could look something like this: Players: 5 women/3 male characters

Helene Kramer (called Leni) - widow (70 years old). Rudolf Pleiss - Rudolf's son from his first marriage (40-50 years). Ina Pleiss was Rudolf's wife from his second marriage (approx 40-50 years). Daniel Pleiss (both sons - 20-25 years). Additionally Helga Willms, Leni's close friend was approximately 60 Years. Trude Lehmann also played an integral part. Karl-Heinz Arens was present throughout this period -70 years).
Gabi Meyer (20-25 Years).

As our play requires five female and three male actors, this combination should prove versatile for use across many stages. Karl-Heinz and Gabi still remain open roles - their relationship with Leni is still developing as we write. When selecting Leni's friends I opted for multiple ages because many stages do not feature three players who are all already 70 years old together - in addition to providing humorous dialogue between characters who all hold distinct perspectives due to age disparity.
Character and Appearance Description of Characters

Now that the protagonists have been chosen, you can take time to describe each character on the following page. While some authors do this step explicitly, I prefer for dialogue to lead me directly into character development - otherwise my piece probably wouldn't work so well. Characters exist solely within your head. Conflict added early creates different types of people with distinct character traits; similarly clothing descriptions should describe who appears. Clothing also depends on character. If it makes more sense for you to visualize your characters on page 5, feel free to do so. On that same page under their names please write the playing time, location and possibly duration of the piece - publishers and groups appreciate this gesture immensely! That could look something like this:

Playtime and location for this play: Summer in Blumberg (small village somewhere in Germany).
Playing Time: Approx. 100 Minutes Without Breaks
The playing time of your piece depends entirely on you; some works have also been developed around specific festivals like Christmas, Easter or Pentecost; this then determines its season automatically. Of course, if your piece spans multiple seasons, the seasons also shift accordingly. For example: If Act 1 of her play begins in February; child birth takes place during Act 2, which takes place August or September; This information is essential, since actors will likely wear different clothing during winter and August respectively, and you can add more climate-based dialogue into the dialogue. I would prefer that our play be set exclusively in summer; I don't yet know the duration, but no more than 4-6 weeks should suffice - or one summer may suffice.

Setting: My inspiration for this piece with its charming little grocery store comes from images of small villages - both urban and rural.
Where your piece takes place doesn't really matter; all that matters is that its audience recognizes quickly that this small place and the nearest town are only kilometers apart. I prefer creating fictional venue names; real places rarely make their appearance in my work. Some groups even like to adjust the action to where their performance actually is taking place if necessary; I don't mind; our venue in Blumberg sounds just like a village anyway!

Playtime depends on the length of pages. For example, choosing size 12 Times New Roman typeface and DIN A5 as page sizes would produce something like the dialog example on page 61 of this book - however I recommend inserting paragraphs between dialogues for added impact. With this format, 90 pages of text equal about 90 minutes of pure playback; tip: an ideal piece should not exceed 120 minutes without breaks - 90 is ideal.
The 100 minutes stated in the description are non-binding and serve only as an example.
What should be included on the first few pages is an outline of your content, yet that may not be possible yet because we don't yet know it all; at least not me! But if you do know, I applaud you and encourage you to write it all down immediately.

CHAPTER SEVEN: BEGINNING

Word processing programs give us the power to add and delete text at will and to change layout at any time, just as publishers do before printing your manuscript. I suggest setting up the pages for your piece now at least; some publishers use DIN A4, while some prefer DIN A5. Ultimately it is up to you which format works for your piece initially - you can always switch formats later on!
Assuming you want a change, set the pages up with DIN A5, starting on page 5. On that page you begin writing the first act; cover pages 2-4 contain titles/authors/content/players and stage design details; all that's really needed to set up pages is a tabulator with names of characters on left edge and dialogue tabulated so it is easier for actors to learn - like this:

Beatrice: Paula, take a different perspective: you're single and need support of some sort - at 55, that means living off one income alone...

Paula: Thank you for reminding me about my extraordinary life!

Beatrice: Why bother taking a vacation, when all it will do is provide temporary respite in Merseburg and you have zero talent with picking out Christmas presents?

Paula: Hold on! My sister Gertrud's children wait eagerly every year for presents from Aunt Paula; that is three of them aged 12, 15 and 21 - I know what demands young people make in terms of gifts (eats again). (Paula has to pause)

Beatrice: Christmas gifts this year may be smaller.

Paula: Yes, exactly 50 percent smaller. - Do you care what they are doing to us here?! Why are you always behaving this way - PIANO?

Beatrice: Because there's no point in being angry over things we as average citizens cannot affect. For instance, Germany's economy faces stiff competition, while other European nations can produce chocolate more cost effectively - that is just how things work.
Paula: Hello... Can I have your perspective for this meeting of all company employees...? Paula:

Have you completed that step? Great. Now choose an easily legible typeface; Times New Roman and Arial are popular options. If all this is causing problems and you are new to WORD or you need further instructions from me, I can only offer basic guidance; my book would not provide in-depth explanations on how to use a word processing program like Word. Hence the best option may be getting someone experienced to teach you its basics or taking a course in WORD.

On page 5, you are writing "ACT FIRST. 3-act acts are extremely popular among theater groups, and I prefer writing plays in this form myself. The number of acts depends heavily on how often or if at all your work requires time-jumping; since this will likely be your initial effort, it would probably make the most sense to begin with a 3-acter. First come the descriptions of how the first scene when curtain opens comes together: do characters enter? or is no one there yet and we only hear noise? In "Welcome to Chez Andre," written together with Christoph Bredau it all looks something like this:

First Act. (When the curtain opens, Andre and Frank are sitting around a table reading an edition of a daily newspaper while looking slightly downcast. There's a cell phone on the table; it is Tuesday afternoon with objects scattered about such as clothes, newspapers, empty bottles and food packages).
Do not exaggerate, but imagine two people dressed sloppily (T-shirts or open shirts without buttons, jeans with cracks and worn sneakers, old sneakers). They don't appear very tidy. They appear to have mixed shoes. They appear not very tidy with each other either - not quite tidy but not dirty either - when walking towards one another in an "ill-mannered manner").

So you need to give details of who's present, what they are doing and which props may still be needed in a scene. When describing clothes of actors as well as mood/behavior/time of day can all help create the impression the viewer gets of everything they see at once: entire stage set plus first scene - immediately inform him/her without needing dialogue from actors themselves!
What would I think if I described the beginning of "Welcome to Chez Andre" like I did before in just 10-20 seconds as a viewer?
I can envision two men, neither dressed very neatly, reading newspapers at a table together while appearing bored and sitting there reading them both while looking rather bored - an instantaneous understanding for any viewer! This scene should be clear to everyone right?

As soon as your audience begins thinking, your piece begins its first dialogue. No need for lengthy prefaces and introductions; start directly from this initial situation. As a viewer, I can already tell that something is wrong between both characters; their interactions seem uneasy, leaving an audience member knowing something of this yet wordless scene. - Another example could be:

At the start of Act 1 (Maundy Thursday approx 16.30 o'clock), there will be no players on stage when the curtain opens; instead there are only flowers with withered petals sitting wiltedly on flower stools and windowsills, along with television sets covered by sheets or cloths and possibly other objects covered with cloth coverings.)

Here, the initial situation is more unusual. No player on stage. Withered flowers and covered pieces of furniture are all present; what should the viewer make of all this? Are there people hiding here? It certainly looks that way...
No one has been there in a while - we don't know whether the apartment is empty, or its inhabitants away traveling - but the audience will learn quickly in the first scene and dialogue that follows. One fact not revealed through text: It is Maundy Thursday; however, soon enough this becomes known through dialogue that follows. - Third example:

Harald is sitting at his desk, typing away on his computer keyboard; Lena vacuums dust in front of him; Harald seems annoyed by its noise while Lena appears distressed by it all and constantly wipes her tears away - all this on an ordinary Saturday morning morning!
At curtain rise we find two lively actors on stage; a man and woman. Although it remains unknown whether these two are married or life partners yet; nonetheless we see evidence of conflict without words being exchanged - with him annoyed by the sound of his vacuum cleaner; she appearing very distressed by it all. No additional props (except perhaps for that same vacuum cleaner) seem necessary here - in fact the stage design remains unchanged just like previously described.
Once you have described the start of the game, begin dialogue immediately in the first scene of Act 1. Some authors who try their first novel make the mistake of writing lengthy dialogue as an opening introduction; this can be tedious and awkward. Instead, move straight to action immediately in Scene 1 with no unnecessary preambles, as relationships and conflict should appear naturally during playing.
As an audience member, I frequently experience directors stepping out in front of the curtain and welcoming us before explaining and describing the piece - sometimes down to every last detail and including an eventual punchline. At these moments I

could go up on stage and kill this person immediately; someone must first explain everything for me!

As much as I want to watch right now, the content must be so poorly written or this person so incompetent as to necessitate this requirement.

He does this because he assumes his audience lacks enough intelligence to appreciate comedy. A third possibility could be that so much text has been cut out that an explanation is necessary; as a spectator, however, I must comprehend all elements without needing announcements and explanations from an official.

So what could the opening scene of your play look like? Now that we understand its central concept, you have several choices available to you for setting off the action of the story. Consider these possibilities: 1. No players on stage but we hear Leni saying goodbye to a customer before coming in the living room immediately afterwards. 2. Leni and her children sit around a table. 3. Leni introduces Daniel her grandson into the living room.

4. Leni is in her store when her son and daughter-in-law enter, discussing its future alongside that of Leni's store and her own.

So there are various ways you can start the action moving, but ultimately the choice lies with you. Conflict is the foundation of all comedy plays, so when setting one in place it should emerge within five minutes or rapidly develop in act one - making for an exciting, entertaining play! In our case this meant providing quick updates about what Leni's children were up to quickly enough.

Every now and again I receive manuscripts from young writers looking for my honest opinion before offering it to publishers. Although dramaturgically correct plays are subjective matters of taste, I can still provide first-time writers with honest advice regarding any serious errors in their manuscripts or lack thereof. When reading work like two or three actors have an agreeable conversation in which all parties involved simply nod along or agree without disagreement and the viewer starts wondering what's going on it's definitely not good writing; something needs to happen or it must at least leave them thinking this way!

On stage, nothing of interest should happen without conflict! Remember this phrase: "No Conflict Is Appropriate!!!!". Therefore, here is how our piece could begin in its first scene:

Rudolf and Ina stand silently in the room when the curtain opens; both look unsure and uncertain. Leni can be heard bidding farewell to one of their customers from behind).

If we choose this route, the audience will immediately become immersed in the drama's first scene. While you might already anticipate Rudolf and Ina wanting to meet Leni, let's change things up: What about this instead:
(When the curtain opens, there is no player present on stage. Leni then steps forward from behind with a cash box, sits down at a table and begins counting money; shortly thereafter Daniel enters from the right.)
Now we learn about Leni and her shop, meet Daniel, and can allow the conflict to emerge later - how fast the audience encounters that conflict is up to you; what matters is that it occurs at all.

A play typically comprises multiple acts. In the first act, we set up conflict while providing audience information about characters; during act two we develop plot elements further and reach climaxes; finally in act three we clarify conflict and bring it all to an end - fulfilling most characters while leaving an enjoyable viewing experience for viewers alike.

Each piece in our play features not only a main plot but can also contain subplots. Leni and her shop serve as our main plot; additional subplots could involve Rudolf being attracted to Daniel or vice versa or possibly Leni having marital problems.

Before writing your first act, I want to point out an error I often see among manuscripts sent by young writers: they often make the mistake of breaking up romantic couples too early or simply not giving enough character development in general. Under no circumstance should this occur:

Acts typically run for 25-35 minutes in duration (if your three or four act play is long enough) without any time shifts; so if the breakfast table scene starts at 8 am and finishes by 8:30 am then that act has concluded at 8:30 am. Start the second act around 3 pm in the afternoon, and it should end by around 3:30 p.m. This should make time real during your game act; however if time shifts occur unavoidably (e.g. due to actors getting in/out at different times), smart solutions must be found (e.g. introducing multiple acts and different scenes simultaneously). Change from evening to morning using music and light effects so the viewer is aware of these time shifts. Preferably this should occur during an appropriate break with no actors present on stage; but in general it would be wiser not to do this. Between acts, time can be played with as you see fit - this could include minutes, hours, days, weeks, months and years! Just don't change time in a single act! I have read manuscripts and seen plays where the first act starts at breakfast and ends 25 minutes later when the main character goes to a disco that opened its doors at 8 AM! And yet the dialogue usually indicates it was late evening by then - how am I meant to comprehend that scenario as a viewer? Don't make this kind of mistake!

As you write, keep each character at the forefront of your mind as you write. Where is she right now - what are her intentions? This will prevent Leni from entering the bedroom then coming back out later as an outsider; she must have entered through some other means if that were the case and there wasn't a rhyme or reason given in the play for such action; otherwise the viewer might become confused and bewildered. - This same technique works when writing flash fiction as well.

Duration of absence refers to how long actors' absences last; for example, when characters make large purchases they should allot sufficient time and allow the audience to follow along as best they can. Keep an eye out for any minute details which might slip past; viewers have very keen eyes which notice everything and everything can be noticed by them very easily; so when an actor leaves the room to go shopping they cannot come back in two minutes with full bags. Think about how long YOU need for shopping; give this actor enough screen time in your piece or let them appear again if necessary.

As you write the first act, be mindful that every line spoken by your characters must convey meaning. Ask yourself why an actor says something. Don't know exactly what this actor means by it? Look:
Anne: (after some deliberation) What do you think about our new tea service? Florian: Mother and father purchased it to commemorate mother's sister's 20th wedding anniversary; at least six cups were purchased directly by mother herself from Purple Flowers Tea Party Shoppe (Burwood Road). Anne:
Florian: Something beautiful on the wall will last a lifetime, Anne replied in disdain. What kind of motif was intended? A naked woman for her bedroom perhaps? Florian may like something similar (smiling)
Anne: Yes, of course - let's just forget about that quickly - the ideal present should be something unexpected that won't simply please Father. Florian: Why must gifts for parents' silver wedding anniversary be distinctive and oddball? Anne: Well, because we are the children - surely this should not be too difficult?
Florian: What do you think... - Mom has been complaining for weeks about how her pots keep on burning. Anne: That is an unacceptable wedding present from children! They do not give household appliances and pots.
Florian: Sure. Better something practical than something they won't use than something pointless like some form of useless trinkets or toys that they won't ever use again. Anne: No thanks - that would never do! If my husband gave me something practical like an egg cooker or toaster on our wedding day I wouldn't marry that either!

As can be seen clearly, a sibling couple are discussing an appropriate present for their parents on their silver wedding anniversary, however neither agree on an ideal solution - one son prefers practical considerations while the other wishes for romance and wants it done right. Through dialogue, we learn much about both characters - each sentence being meaningful in itself giving insight to who said what and when!

Reducing unnecessary details just because your scene should be longer is key; keep on track by staying focused; in time you will get this under control, but at first keep asking "Why does Character X say or react this way?" and "Why did Character Y respond like that?" as prompts.

As a follow up to my earlier suggestion, let me suggest how our comedy could begin in its initial scene:

1. Leni: (entering from the rear of the store with her cash box and book, she walks directly towards a table and sits down. Once there she begins counting money and writing numbers down in her book before becoming overwhelmed and giving up counting altogether). Her clothing appears normal and everyday).

2. Scene 2 Daniel (he comes in from the right, wearing summery sports clothes and knocks shortly beforehand. Leni is pleased to see her grandson) Daniel! My boy! Daniel: (goes up and gives Leni a kiss on the cheek), then asks how business went today before giving a compliment about sales, was everyone satisfied?

Leni: As for my needs, they are always met and no longer refer to me as Aunt Emma.

Daniel: Grandma Leni, can I have another pack of cigarettes please? Its Leni: Smoking too frequently...

Daniel: (interrupts her) Smoking harms your health, ages the skin, can reduce impotence and stinks...- Grandma, quitting isn't that easy... Leni: Your grandfather felt exactly the same way back then; he couldn't keep his hands off of smoking either and that was at only 73 years old!

Daniel: Grandma, I need you to help. Your Grandfather had an accident. mes Leni: (slightly sad) Yes. Let's not talk about it; just help yourself. Daniel (strokes her shoulder briefly, before leaving to assist his store partner at the back) Leni (looks up at him briefly before continuing her accounting work)

Third Scene

Ina and Rudolf walk in wearing summer clothing. Rudolf greets Ina briefly as Ina makes a direct and assertive entrance: Good evening mother-in-law! Rudolf responds quickly: Mother.

Leni: (slightly startled) Yikes, you? I was still doing the daily billing when you came in here! What can I offer you, a tea?

Ina: [with purpose and firmness] Mother-in-law, please come sit down again because there's something going on between us that we must discuss. Leni sat back down tentatively unsure what's happening or why Ina is so serious-faced. Ina continued speaking her mind with determination: You seem very serious today Ina! Ina's tone was clear when she came in while standing up slowly after finally sitting back down again: Yes? So what's up today Ina? But you seem so serious! So what gives Ina so serious? And so what happens with her serious expression? She looks quite serious to

Leni as she slowly sits back down again unsure, uncertainly sits slowly back down again: Yes? So what are we talking about today Ina? Ina is obviously looking so intense. Leni, uncertainly sits back down slowly: Yes? So what's happening here today Ina? Leni slowly sits down again: Yes? So what's going on here today Ina?
Leni slowly sits back down again: Oh? So what is happening today with your expression? Ina
Rudolf: Mother, we wanted to talk with you for weeks now but kept postponing it. Ina: But now it is too late; we cannot wait any longer. Leni: That sounds dramatic. Have I done something wrong? 4th Scene.
Daniel: (returning from the back of the store during Ina's last sentence; holding a pack of cigarettes and looking around) Oh - family reunion?
Ina: What are you doing here? I think you must be at football training.
Daniel: Canceled (foreshadows evil). Your look tells me something is amiss here... It appears you're not here for coffee, Rudolf. Daniel: That isn't right; no way, not like this! Leni: Who are they talking to now?
Rudolf: How long are we carrying this around with us? Daniel: Dad. Leni: Wow. So this is it; are you telling me I must close down my shop and move into an assisted retirement community! - Well now the truth has been revealed.

As soon as the piece begins this way, conflict is inevitable within minutes. You've already provided plenty of insight into Leni's character - widow; relationships with grandson good; wanting to interrupt accounting to offer something to children; Daniel knows about what their parents plan - yet seems disapproves; son- and daughter-in-law seem harsh towards Leni; they both don't like her presence - all within three pages of text!

However, we could also wait until Ina and Rudolf come into view first. Perhaps you prefer it better if Daniel told his grandmother what his parents were planning, or it may even be that Leni's girlfriend saw Ina and Rudolf have planned for Leni and so was the first person to enter the scene - anything is possible here - take what you like or find your own unique starting point; your piece belongs to you!
Let's go ahead with my suggestion - what could the piece entail next? Now is your opportunity! How does Leni respond and what does she do next? Daniel could offer his help for Leni at this point; for how long does this conversation continue; who leaves and who enters next scene?
What will become of Leni and her shop? This must be the theme that unifies your entire comedy - right up until its conclusion. Let your imagination run wild as you write out every possible scenario - here are a few helpful hints:

Avoid writing dialogues lasting more than 10 minutes that consist merely of an endless dialogue without high or low points, as this quickly becomes boring for viewers. Something should always be happening; build tension. Fill one act of your comedy with at least 8 scenes; more may sometimes work better. Do not attempt to make people in the audience laugh with crude expressions in dialogue - comedy should come from dialogue, text and situational comedy alone, not using piggy words to encourage viewers to "thigh-tap".

Questioning what constitutes true humor may leave you asking: what exactly amusing am I watching, the audience laughing about? First rule of comedy is this: the audience knows more than any actor on stage about what's going on!!

Dramaturgically correct work must begin with an understanding of tension and comedy at work simultaneously. You know what I mean?

Imagine that when someone is hiding in a room but the other people present don't notice him/her; while an audience member knows. All this creates both tension and comedy simultaneously.

"Those who dig a pit for others will fall into it themselves" Anyone familiar with this expression knows it well - setting traps for others in order to pull them down into one can lead them down into it themselves - whether this takes the form of poisonous drinks, altered foodstuffs, rat traps or letters or telephone conversations etc...

At first glance, this seems hilarious for both viewer and character. At any rate, this type of scenario usually works well in comedies: viewers laugh when a completely different character or even the one setting the trap themselves falls for it, making for great comedic irony. Mistaken identities tend to go over well too - both objects and people can easily become confused!

Have a house, an appointment and various other necessities.

Misunderstandings in conversations can also be hilarious: when Character A mentions his ship Antje, Character B may assume he means his wife with the same name - deliciously funny reverse factor comedies are always welcome! Trend - from 2008:

How is that happening? A man acts like a woman or vice versa for unknown reasons. What factors could explain such behaviors?

For example: Manner acting like prostitutes? Men doing striptease. And women can even become bricklayers!

Or a woman as Chancellor (unfortunately already exists). These are just some suggestions, many of which I have already included into my pieces; there are even more! Doing these things cleverly and correctly will only lead to laughter-inducing results in comedy pieces.

Create something nonexistent in real life.

On stage, this can make for very funny viewing:

A representative offers products that were once unavailable - permanent wave preparations that last months; hair growth products with extreme fast growth effects; panty liners for men; chocolates that increase intelligence rapidly, etc - that were previously unavailable for purchase - however unfortunately these have many side effects and it could quickly turn disastrous! My performance entitled "We Don't Have It - It Doesn't Exist" focused specifically on this theme.

Or take medical innovation. An amateur chemist creates a serum to completely eliminate sweat odor, making this wonderful invention obsolete and unnecessary odorousness of sweat ever again - but needs volunteers to test this with and its highly concentrated hormones will alter people. ("The Crazy Professor"). All such topics may seem ridiculous but have an enormous influence on society at large.

Funny characters in comedies are always very effective. By "funny character," I mean that.

These figures often stand out from their fellow characters in various ways, be it flaws or otherwise. Examples could include things such as language errors (not speaking German or a dialect); awkward or less educated individuals; actors of color; those dressed differently and other things. Such characters add character and often become audience favorites quickly. Furthermore, such "funny characters" need not play major roles to add humor; even minor ones in subplots can prove just as entertaining!

*Personally, I do not favour including characters with speech impediments in the play. Your characters should all be unique; otherwise where will drama and conflict stem from?

Language and expression is an extremely sensitive issue. Watch any film from the 70s with Theo Lingen or Roy Black; wasn't that fun? But, seriously - are you as excited by their plots and dialogue as when they first released (if you're under 30 you won't know them anyway; rent them from your video store and judge). I only find these films funny rarely now as what's shown is often not very "funny". Time has certainly altered everything.

Nowadays when watching an evening program film on television, we tend to see more skin exposed compared to films from the 1970s. Not only that; contemporary movies certainly need to reflect this shift as much of it happens verbally - think "Sex and the city", which features at least 50 sexual words not part of my everyday vocabulary nor yours!

What distinguishes entertainment from television series or films such as TV play films from stage plays in terms of language use and visual freedom?

No one can give you an exact answer here either; theater on stage is always live! Your next question might be what can and cannot be shown or said onstage; I refer here specifically to what has been written up as script and must then be reproduced by actors onstage.

Well, theater is an extensive field. Actors appear completely bare-chested in some plays - expressing everything they can. I primarily specialize in popular theater productions run by amateur groups.

No amateur actor I know would appear in an amateur folk play dressed only in black undergarment; and, as an audience member, this would not be something that appeals to me either. Plus it just seems weird.

Love and sex are perennial topics in popular theater, so I enjoy having images in my mind of what might be going on next door. For instance, an empty stage next to which there is an open door with male voices from either gender; some time later when someone comes onto stage wearing their briefs slightly sweaty but satisfied, everyone can create their own versions of what happened there instead of seeing something real happen and shown live onstage. I find this much more engaging.

As I discussed it during the debate, my thinking on this was similar. While amateur actors today may use words such as "blow," "bum," and "fuck," there's nothing inherently wrong with writing your play that way if it seems necessary; however, most actors would use different terminology when performing for an audience.

I don't use these words at all in my pieces! This topic has already generated heated conversations, with people questioning my overly formal pronunciation in dialogues of my plays. But here's my explanation:

"Bumping etc." is not part of my everyday language. As an audience member in a theater watching a comedy performance, I want to be completely engaged by what's happening; living along with the actors; I also create images in my mind of things happening off stage as told to me by them - when someone wants to go shopping or take a shower; for instance; this happens instantly in my mind!

At first, it may sound surprising but spoken dialogue has this same effect on me; when an actor tells me they killed a cat or someone reported they robbed a bank, I imagine these images. Reading novels creates similar effects as your mind visualises characters, places, objects and events from a novel into your imagination.

If one of the actresses on stage were to say: "Oh, I would like to do it uninhibitedly with my boss at the kitchen table," I'd immediately have an image in mind and laugh out loud at their words. However, what would happen if instead they said: "Oh, I want to fuck my boss" instead?

As a viewer, I would be shocked. Shock moments can be powerfully impactful in many pieces; however, they will never appear in my works as viewers prefer having fun and creating their own images in their heads over being shocked by someone on stage through dialogue.

That is my viewpoint on it; however, should yours differ, no laws exist to stop you.

Question of Play Limit? I have written comedies featuring women who are deeply attracted to men that contain some very spicy content; their actors can take off clothing as part of their role; even I may strip down to my underwear when necessary! But perhaps the following scenes could take place in another room nearby instead?

If you go further and use extremely crude language, your audience will feel as though they are witnessing a real life smear theater performance.

Your comedy should meet a certain standard and level. Find an appropriate level of eroticism and let it unfold naturally - don't bombard your audience with verbal abuse; this tactic is unnecessary and unnecessary.

At the conclusion of each act, make it so exciting that audiences cannot wait to see how your comedy unfolds next. At each act's close, ensure the plot reaches new climaxes.

When writing, always consider your reader when considering information needed by characters on stage. And do not overlook game instructions in dialogue - which should appear between parentheses; these instructions will be invaluable to actors!

Gerda:

Correct! Where has Manni been? He should have finished milking by now - it's almost 8 pm (goes to backdoor and calls his name:) Manni!!! (comes back, spreads bread & butter onto plate, tops it off with cheese etc)

Arno: (reads the magazine with interest) And this means we won't need to do the cleaning ourselves anymore?

Heinrich: Oh no! Everything seems to have vanished into the canal.

Arno: Just take a look at how much space cows occupy.

Heinrich: Yes! They will feel comfortable there and produce better milk as a result.

Gerda: Why would more space lead to producing higher-quality milk?

Heinrich: Gerda, how often have you complained of discomfort when wearing your old girdle?

Gerda: Hello beautiful!!!

Arno: (laughing) For ease of understanding, I have written my playing instructions here in italics to facilitate learning by the actor on stage from you - the author. They must learn not only what their lines will be but also gestural requirements such as when to leave or enter etc. Don't omit playing instructions altogether but be wary not overdo your execution either!

Back to my original idea: the comedy with Leni, her shop and children who want to deport them to a nursing home. If this idea appeals to you and would like you to write about it, let your imagination run wild about what could happen!
Please feel free to send me your first writing attempts; I will review and reply honestly. On my website www.Theater-Schmidt.de you will find my contact details under Legal Notice.

After watching numerous classic plays (particularly those by female writers), viewers already know from their first conflict between a young woman and man that "in the end they'll get each other!" Why do authors do that? Because audiences like seeing an "happily ever after" ending at the end, or because the author wants to create one? I have done this myself in many pieces because I know from previous pieces what comes next - although not in all my recent pieces!

My writing has distancing myself somewhat from it; not everything must end well - which may even be unrealistic - so don't think initially that two young characters who initially dislike each other, yet come together at the end of a play, can end up together by falling into each other's arms at its conclusion. While this could happen, just write your story; "peace, joy and pancakes" don't always exist in real life!

Not to misunderstand; viewers would ideally like to walk away with most of the play's inconsistencies resolved or at least have an idea as to what might develop after its conclusion, while any conflicts should be clarified; even if this means reaching an accommodation with all those involved; but find a satisfactory resolution that leaves an audience satisfied. Do you remember my comedy "Praxis Dr. Freeseman?"

Harald Freesemann has spent years writing books that, due to lack of publisher interest, remain unpublished. So his wife Lena must make ends meet as their cleaning lady until one day a new tenant moves in on the floor above them and requires her services as cleaning lady as well. Gisela reports that Gisela has found an individual she refers to as a "brain plumber." Coincidentally, his last name is Freesemann - something Lena and Harald find disturbing since they now anticipate disruption from patients of his. Dr. Horst Freesemann would normally insist they go past the first floor if they wanted treatment from him, but Harald had already entered through one of the doors and is currently inside Harald's room. Harald recognizes his opportunity and begins treating this man who desperately wants treatment and eagerly puts a few hundred euros on the table for it. But then an actual psychiatrist suddenly appears, wanting Harald to treat them both because they both suffer from endogenous psychosis...

This piece may end in chaos, but viewers won't leave feeling dissatisfied: its protagonist has had his financial worries resolved through writing a manuscript about what transpired on stage alongside him.

Harald was inspired to write this play by his wife, and is having it published. A neighbor found out that Harald was treating patients despite not being licensed doctor; their outrage was silenced by a trip. Unfortunately, none of the mentally ill characters in this play are ever cured - on the contrary; all "normal" ones eventually go crazy too!

Dramaturgically speaking, everything works well: the main conflict has been resolved while new ones may arise; therefore, the piece can end on an upbeat note, leaving both viewer and characters satisfied but concerned for what could come next.
We all recognize this experience from movies or TV. How often have we watched an exciting film only for it to abruptly end...?
Producers and screenwriters frequently utilize this approach when telling a tale; they outline its story, attempt to address its main problem while only indirectly concluding it. Although similar strategies don't apply in theatre performance settings, producers and screenwriters do use similar strategies when telling their tale.
But if you prefer giving your play a happy ending, that is perfectly acceptable - I just wanted to make you aware of the fact that there are no hard and fast rules!

Publishers and groups require you to present the contents of your piece on the first pages of your manuscript, whether that's before writing begins or midway through or after finishing an act. Publishers typically don't alter this element of a play's presentation - theatre groups frequently use this description of their play for advertisements in flyers, program booklets and press. Please make your content engaging but no more than one DIN A5 page long! Would you like some examples on how it might look like? - here's some help:

Alida Neumann no longer finds any meaning in her marriage to Ingo and wants to end it by taking sleeping pills. Due to Ingo's wrong shares and too-large house purchase, their financial troubles have spiraled out of control and they now owe over 300,000 euros together. Alida suspects Ingo of having an affair as he has recently received many letters and calls from women. To protect himself financially from potential lawsuits arising from these relationships, Ingo requested Alida obtain four life insurance policies worth 150,000 euros each from her life insurers. Alida believes she should be murdered by Ingo and thus resorts to suicide as her plan falls through; but Ingo comes up with something far different - advertising in various newspapers for photo models who could come visit his place and inviting them in person. Alida and Ingo hope to go abroad after creating an image of Alida as closely as possible - at least in terms of height and weight. Ingo plans on drugging Alida before driving her down a steep hill with her in his wife's car so as to claim on life insurance policies in case an accident takes place; later they plan to collect insurance money together through fake accidents. - Ingo has found his perfect victim in Gabi Koch. However, Ingo quickly falls in love with Gabi and changes their plan by wanting to put Alida into their car instead. Shortly before her planned murder, Gabi discovers through Alida that Ingo intended for her to be murdered and is shocked at this news. Soon thereafter, Alida and Gabi enjoy each other as much as discovering love for each other before hatching a plan to eliminate Ingo with poisoned cola that accidentally gets drunk by Sven (Ingo's friend) instead of killing Ingo herself... With Else Krautwurst coming forward... The body must find somewhere quickly to bury itself.

As you read through a piece, don't reveal its ending until the very last sentence has been read aloud; that will create interest among game directors, making the piece more likely to get printed without readers having seen its end before printing it themselves. Also consider this suggestion:

Anna Thalmann is the mother of an 18-year-old daughter and lives with one husband who works away during the week and earns "good wages", plus two "best friends" whom she spends time with on one or two days each week.

She shares hours of gossip, as well as confided her most intimate matters to a bird that is trusted with keeping tabs on them both. Her rental apartment is large and well furnished, while she has never experienced serious illness herself; all indications point towards being an exceptional woman. Her daily struggles have left her feeling useless and abandoned by her family in her role of caring mother and wife. Erwin has an unhealthy attitude toward his wife; when home on weekends he prefers watching football games or attending his skat game rather than spending time with her. Anna has started to internalise her frustration by indulging in excessive eating - something which has resulted in being 20 kilograms overweight. But now, Anna wants to change something! She orders fitness equipment from a TV shop, attends gymnastics group sessions and gets make-up advice from Sonja - all while hoping to rekindle the flame in her marriage with ease and speed. However, their plan remains complex and complicated. One day when Anna's washing machine breaks down, Mustafa Yldiz arrives to repair it - and is immediately entranced by Anna. He invites her over for an unforgettable "Turkish" evening! Will Anna succumb to his charms or take control of her life herself?

Here, too, we uncover content and conflict without being privy to its resolution. Similarly, your pieces should follow suit.

As every play requires a title, naming one can sometimes be challenging. An ideal title should reveal something about the show while simultaneously being captivating to audience members when reading posters and program booklets. Titles may consist of just one word, be a question or contain whole sentences; I generally advise against long titles though and prefer more vague versions like the following as examples:

Rita and Ulfert Brauer, who are extremely wealthy individuals, recently relocated from the city to the countryside with their son Heiner. Your neighbours.

Diekmann couple Heiko (worker) and Gesine (housewife) live a "simple" existence despite living in poor conditions; though they must make sacrifices here and there to survive; yet remain healthy and content with life. Rita (beautician) and Ulfert (editor-in-chief) make their presence felt daily to their neighbors as evidence that they are superior. An argument ensues between families when Marion Diekmann returns home from Alabama. As an au pair in Germany for one year, she shocked everyone when she returned - initially to everyone's chagrin - by introducing Jonny, an African medical student! This proved too much for the Brauer couple. Both families are now trying to make life difficult for each other through nasty intrigues and attacks, leading to court settlements; eventually a high fence was installed between their properties to separate them further. When Gesine attacks Ulfert again, Ulfert suffers a heart attack, yet Jonny alone can save his life...

Content wise, the story's plot is pretty clear. At its heart lies two very different families and we see their differences both character- and financial-wise. That is exactly what I attempted to portray in my title - so here you will find it all.
Viewers two very stark contrasts are highlighted here by my title; which can be roughly translated as: "Mettwurst Bread and Caviar". No actor will eat either item directly; this distinction between them only exists through their titles.
Menno and Mathilde Gruben return from a 4-week vacation in Egypt with their two children Henning and Anette eagerly awaiting Easter celebrations; but instead find that upon their return a pile of reminders from utility companies has arrived in their mailbox and call to the bank confirms an account overdrawn by 30,000 euros; an incorrect booking may have contributed to this error, so bank employees are eager to resolve it as soon as they return from holidays.

In this play, a family is challenged to live self-sufficiently for one week without even intending it. So what could the title of this piece be?
"Robinson Crusoe sends his regards". That fits, doesn't it?!
And one last example:
Contents: Nico and Silvia Schroder celebrate their first wedding anniversary. Nico is delighted that his wife did not leave him, even though he has been unemployed for an entire year and Silvia must earn support for both of them. Nico reads an attractive job offer from a coffee company in his daily newspaper and quickly applies by phone and is quickly accepted for employment. But instead of receiving promised samples of coffee, instead erotic magazines arrive unexpectedly at his house a few days later, leaving Nico baffled at how to explain this discrepancy. Silvia is furious with Nico; she believes he needs a replacement due to her pregnancy. Things only worsen as his mother-in-law moves in as well, having serious issues with him. Nico thinks everything has been resolved until ERO shows up; then everything becomes unclear again.

This title combines the initial letters of two companies involved in this piece - an exclusive romantic oasis and Timann coffee - into one word to form "ERO-TI-KA". Since sex is at the core of this comedy, this title makes perfect sense.
Ingo Sax has written an extremely clever play about a young woman suffering from mutism - the inability to communicate or make contact. Called "Amanita", its main actress Celia has become famous due to this role in this four-person production by

Ingo Sax - so take a look and you will soon understand why the author chose that name! Thank you to Ingo Sax for his incredible feat!

Don't overthink deciding on a title; "The Inn of the Golden Anchor", "Jubilaum", "The Star of Padua", and "The Smuggling Brothers", among many other popular and often award-winning plays have titles that simply refer to where an event took place or describe what made it tick - that is perfectly acceptable!
But some stage works have boring titles as well. One piece I know simply called "Theater" leaves little room for imagination or creativity when considering its dramaturgy or content.
Once your work is completed, or while writing it, determining its name may come naturally; but I would like to conclude the discussion surrounding title selection by outlining some options available to us when considering one for your play.
Imagine this: Sometimes when I'm talking with friends, random words or sentences come out that would make great titles for poems or novels.

Consider this. When we read or listen to titles like these, something entirely new emerges. No longer do we begin by formulating an idea and plot before assigning a title later (the way most plays progress); rather we now start from just having the title itself - then create our story around that idea from there! When I see these titles I immediately think of 100 things they could possibly cover - can't you too?
Feel free to try this variant as well, just please avoid using titles I've written here since I plan on incorporating them in my writing over the coming months.

When writing, one must consider all possible outcomes of their writing efforts. A novelist writes his book for readers who can purchase it in bookstores - publishers and printers are involved here as well; for plays and plays intended to be performed, theater groups would likely perform them and their manuscript would never be purchased anywhere, nor read very easily either way - these factors must all be taken into consideration as one writes their play or novel.

Once your play is finished and you feel proud to present it for publication, submit it to one or more publishers for consideration. I suggest starting out by choosing just one that seems suitable; even though reviews may take some time they will usually include suggestions to revise certain parts of your piece or critique of certain scenes from it by editors; eventually publishers send back manuscripts as they become available.

Your request was out of our consideration - thank you very much". Unfortunately, rejection letters like this do not provide details as to why something like this is no longer an option for them. Don't lose hope right away if this happens; take heart! Repudiation from theater publishers doesn't indicate your work is terrible. Take your time reading it carefully again while placing yourself as the spectator watching on stage; experience what you are experiencing first-hand as an audience member when reading through it and experience its full impact before revising thoroughly before offering it up again to other theater publishers. But I also want to be completely upfront: if your work is rejected without any explanation or comment from an editor, that must mean it was really bad - because every editor takes great pains in explaining what they don't like when overall it seems good. Criticism from publishers makes revision and editing much simpler; so if they say there is no need, just accept their answer and move on with what you were writing. If someone says no need for revision, don't ask why; the publisher knows better. If this happens with multiple publishers, you must eventually come to terms with the fact that what you have written may not be of particularly high quality; perhaps writing is simply not your forte or it just doesn't suit you as an artform. At some point in your writing journey, it's important to be honest with yourself and recognize this fact. While we could speculate about other unexplored talents that lie outside writing itself, the point here is not about that - rather, that you believe you can and want to give it a try!

No matter if it be comedy, drama, farce, crime novel, multi-act play or just short sketch - writing in standard German or a dialect dialect is entirely up to you - the fact remains: your piece must first convince an editor at your chosen publisher that your work is coherent with no errors and has an "exciting" plot; doesn't lose its thread and is playable and suitable for them as well as providing stages where necessary.

Your play must address those who will perform it; otherwise, no publisher would sign it and it will sit gathering dust for years without interest from the stage - and that's the last thing you want!

Assume you get mail from your publisher and find that their editor has gone over your piece and provided feedback regarding changes necessary. But perhaps they also mentioned what needs to be altered so it fits within their program exactly as sent in by you.

How would you respond? - I can imagine it: reading the lines and criticism from an editor you don't know well can often be very direct, causing shock, offence and anger. "The piece is great - what was he thinking?"... All these sentences could become issues for you as finding a publisher for a first novel is often challenging.

Stop thinking like that and becoming offended. An editor is not God - they only offer their opinion - yet you should respect his knowledge about his job as well as accept any criticism aimed at your piece. Be reasonable with yourself when accepting criticism, especially regarding specific points which were criticised. Do what the editor advises despite your objections - in time you will recognize its wisdom!

My 47th piece "Welcome to Chez Andre", co-written with Christoph Bredau and submitted to two publishers for consideration, was rejected due to being too risque. When we read their letter we were stunned - this piece's content can be seen here:

Andre Lambrecht and Frank Wattenfall both lost everything on the stock market and are currently unemployed, renting a 2-room apartment together to keep costs low. Unfortunately, no employment opportunities have presented themselves yet so they have already settled their rent payments.

Their landlady Elfriede Krause issues an ultimatum of one week to find work or pay rent; otherwise she wants them out. Andre has an inspired idea. Together they start offering companion and escort services for women at "Welcome to Chez Andre"; quickly accepted by ladies looking for companionship, meals or massages from them; but things quickly escalate beyond expectations as their landlady Elfriede Krause and Tina try everything they can to stop this activity - yet love continues between them...

Here, the oldest trade is depicted quite humorously with its traditional roles reversed, showing just how far people will go to make money today, while simultaneously showing women are very willing to pay money just to have some quality time with men. Our impression is that this gets under the men's skin, as evidenced by one falling in love with a customer because he can no longer stand receiving payment from her, showing very human behaviour on stage while providing great dramaticturgical entertainment. Furthermore, many scenes were quite intense! However, we were required to "defuse" any scenes which went too far for publishers; and one publisher included this revised version in their program. While we found it disappointing that our original piece wasn't accepted - sometimes editors read according to their mood alone! That being said, it must be dealt with.

Assume you receive such a letter from a publisher.
So you get back to work - not annoyed by your editor's letter, but filled with energy and optimism for creating something much greater - perhaps as you make changes you discover that it has improved dramatically; or perhaps you come to recognize more clearly where errors were made previously.
Put aside two hours for revision; your publisher has read your manuscript and may have pointed out errors; therefore you should only submit it a second time when every single point of criticism has been resolved.

Now let's make things even better: Imagine receiving news that your play will be published for the first time ever - what an incredible feeling that must be. At least you've overcome an immense hurdle and made it this far. Is that considered success? Absolutely - so give yourself permission to feel proud of what has already been accomplished here.
Once your play has been published, there's not much you can do but sign a contract with a publisher (I will cover contracts more in-depth in Chapter 12) and hope they offer your work through catalogs sent directly to theater groups every year or via online publishing platforms like Publisher websites.
Now comes the next challenge - reaching theater groups with your piece. Playgroups often order viewing programs from publishers; wouldn't it be great if game directors found your work interesting enough that many theaters ordered viewing programs from your publisher? Unfortunately, I understand your frustration; unfortunately you won't know which stages viewed your piece; generally (depending on publisher) only after one has selected your work will you find out details such as performance group location and dates for performances.
When your piece is performed for the very first time, we call this an inaugural performance or premiere; and often times you, as its author, are invited to attend this historic momentous occasion. And you shouldn't turn down such an offer! Seeing your characters, story and concept come alive before your very eyes is truly exciting; believe me; I know from experience. Maybe the group doesn't execute your piece quite how expected but whatever the outcome it can only add more drama for all parties involved!

Are You Excited Too? However, if the group reports back that rehearsals were enjoyable and they enjoyed staging the play; press criticism is positive and audience numbers match, then your piece can go ahead as planned and count that as your personal success.

Flip through any bookcase of novels and you will quickly realize there are numerous publishers available; unfortunately playwrights don't have as many choices available to them. But there are theater publishers that publish our plays under very reasonable terms, and some even do it exceptionally well. I think building relationships with editors at these publishing houses is key. At first, it's advisable to browse the available publishers online and determine which one(s) might best accommodate your piece. As I was writing dialect pieces as well as Low German pieces from the beginning, Mahnke Verlag in Verden offered the largest selection of Low German stage plays (www.Mahnke-Verlag.de). Some of my pieces can still be found there today!

But there are also publishers who specialize in Low German works and dialect pieces; since 2008, most of my works have been published by Plausus Theaterverlag in Bonn (www.Plausus.de) both in Low and High German versions.

Searching the internet for publishers will reveal several others, such as Reinehr publishing house in Muhltal (www.Reinehr.de), sales office and publishing house of German playwrights Norderstedt (vertriebsstelle.de) or the Rieder theater publishing house Wemding (Theaterverlag-Rieder.de) among many more. However, certain publishers specialize in certain areas such as children's plays or dramas etc.

I can't tell you which publisher will work best for you; all I can say is that for years now, I have enjoyed working closely with Plausus-Verlag in Bonn and Mahnke-Verlag in Verden.

But I had also had some negative experiences.

What should you consider and prioritize in establishing a theater publishing house? Initially an eight year old led a legal dispute. So what factors are essential in taking decisions regarding theater publishing house ownership?

As an author, it is important to form strong bonds with your editor and the employees at the publisher; any theater groups should not lodge complaints about your publisher. Your work is then transferred to the publisher, who must offer it fairly and treat theater groups fairly and equitably. If a theater group voices criticism against your publisher for the way your play was published, take steps to address it immediately. If your work has not been accepted by stages for multiple years due to quality concerns; however if errors lie with them rather than yourself then feel free to voice this.

Publisher websites speak volumes about their work. Though primarily intended for theater groups, authors should also find easily understandable theater pages to browse with pleasure.
Please take your time browsing websites; just the main page can often reveal much about its publisher.

If I find the opening page of a publishing house with only performance regulations shocking, that speaks volumes about their owner and likely indicates negative feelings towards this publishing house; I do not expect you will also find such publishers appealing; thus it is best to avoid such publishers.

If you are having difficulty choosing which publisher to go with and are having difficulty making up your mind online alone is not enough, call the publisher directly and inquire whether they would even consider publishing your work by phone. Doing this gives another impression; if there is someone unprofessional and rude on the other end of the line then consider whether you would want them treating you that way in future dealings (I have come across people describing themselves as editors for theater publishers yet they spelled "premiere" with an "a". Believe me - It wasn't even lying!).

Find out whether a publisher is appropriate for your manuscript by visiting its website and searching their database of books for publication. For instance, if you have written something in Low German Mahnke, Plausus or VVB would likely be your best options; but do be patient as this process could take some time until an answer arrives back from them. However, some publishers will confirm receipt of your work through mail; others may contact you by phone or email; but if no confirmation comes through after several months have gone by then I would demand my manuscript back from them. Theater publishers seem to claim they receive many manuscripts every day without enough time for response or reply. (Other publishers might claim otherwise.) If you know other playwrights, find out which publishers they work with; in general you only ever commit to one publisher when publishing one piece; subsequent pieces can always be offered elsewhere if desired.

Once you have found a publisher and your manuscript has gained interest, a contract will be drawn up that both parties must sign. Each contract can vary slightly.
Not to worry! Individual publishers won't take notice. What matters more are defining author and publisher rights and obligations; as well as discussing finances and duration.

As the author, it is only appropriate for you to grant the publisher the rights necessary for recording on radio and TV, making a film, and translating into other languages. But you remain the original creator - simply giving away rights of use. If anything in the contract does not meet with your approval, simply notify it and discuss possible modifications - maybe one paragraph or regulation might change accordingly!

Naturally, royalty division is an integral element of any contract and usually the author receives 70% - the publisher 30%.
Duration and termination rights can be an arduous discussion point in contracts, yet I always make sure they include clear details as to duration and rights to cancel (e.g. each December 31st with 3-month notice period and automatic renewal if uncancelled).
Do be wary, though: if there is no information in the contract about its duration and only mention is made of its legal protection period, that means nothing other than that your manuscript falls under copyright - in other words, until after your death (70 years post mortem!). I advise only signing contracts that last 3 to 5 years with automatic renewal every year thereafter - even if termination occurs after 5 years it should be accepted, rather than making yourself subject to commitment until your end of life!

Be sure to provide details regarding the length of the contract!

As I sought a publisher for my first work in 1990, I signed my contract without providing dates or deadlines for performance group leaders to accept my pieces, signing after each one was rejected outright by this publisher. If this happens again and performance group leaders contact you and refuse to perform them because of these contracts - as happened in my case - then your hands will be completely tied by them and this mistake forces you to fight your lawyer for 8 years to get out. Finally on April 1, 2008 we had finally won and got out. It took both strength and nerves.

Be smart: make the choice of an "excellent" publisher!!!

Have you ever wondered how much of an income a playwriting career generates? Well here is your chance to discover this answer honestly - much as soldiers or workers receive wages, playwrights receive royalties through publishers that published your piece.

Money will only become payable once your play has been performed by a theater group and they have settled their accounts with the publisher after its season has concluded. As for when and how soon this money arrives: it could take some time. Some publishers settle accounts with authors instantly following settlement with theater groups while others send royalty statements quarterly - with others even sending annual statements out as needed.

How is This Calculated? Every spectator who attends your play must pay an admission fee. As anyone who visits professional or amateur theater regularly will know, groups vary considerably in terms of frequency of performances, size of auditoriums used and admission prices charged per seat - I know of groups which only show 3 performances in rooms that accommodate 100 audience members for 4 euros each while other perform 40 performances over several weeks that seat 350 guests for around 12 euros each! And so the process continues with no end point!

1. Imagine a theater group performing your play five times for an entry fee of five euros per spectator and it being completely sold-out each time; with total income being 2500 euros from this performance alone and 10% or 250 euros going to publisher; out of this sum 70% would go back to you or 175 euros would go directly back into your pockets as payment from this group.

Why did I write "would"? Well - publishers typically establish a minimum rate per performance that must be paid if income drops below certain amounts, usually around 70 euros in our first example. In this instance, this group would not reach this minimum threshold and would therefore need to pay 70 euros as they wouldn't meet the minimum rate per performance; that means 350 euros would go straight back into publisher coffers while 70 euro of that is worth 245 euro to you (70/20= 245)

I hear many theater groups complain about this regulation; "small" stages in particular tend to find it very disturbing. Yet publishers impose heavy costs without this agreement and would find it almost impossible to survive without this framework; so in turn this also benefits us, authors. Believe me; without this regulation in place all stages would likely only pay 30 or 40 euros per performance instead!

I don't think the stages should complain. No matter how much money is brought in, 90% still ends up staying with their group! That seems fair!

2. Example: Supposing your theater seats 1000 people. Entrance fees per person were 12 euros on 16 different dates when your performance took place; that would total 12,454 spectators watching it.

Sounds nice? Well I wish! Unfortunately I have never received such an amount from a group, but my goal here is simply to illustrate how billing can vary between stages - you could receive as little as 70 euros from one and almost 1000 from another!

If you publish an article written in High German and commission a translator to translate it to Low German or another language, they should of course receive royalties; after all, they've done a lot of work translating it. Their share typically stands at 20%.

Hope you are feeling satisfied, as now you know roughly what your earnings potential could be when making plays.

CHAPTER FOURTEEN: WRITING ALONE OR TOGETHER?

I had already completed 40 multi-act plays when Elke Siemers visited me approximately three years ago to talk about her life again. She's an extraordinary pediatric nurse and theater teacher who tells stories in such an engaging, unique manner that it should always be captured on film. Listening to her stories is truly delightful; years ago we realized we could create incredible tales together. Yes, if we allow our imaginations to run wild for an hour, a complete play can emerge almost instantaneously; unfortunately only in our heads at first. Many ideas have since been abandoned quickly. At some point it became evident to me that she had such an exciting and emotionally charged story to share, many from her personal experience, that I knew it would lead to something.

Now you may be asking how writing together works - "writing together". Up until that point I had encountered two approaches. Elke had already completed numerous works: paintings, performances on stage, poetry writing and short novels writing as well as plays; she even attempted them herself! By then Elke had painted many pictures, written poetry stories short novels but refused dialogue style writing as not being her forte - in her words.

This was my inaugural experience of writing collaboratively. By 2008 spring we collaborated again, this time with Christoph Bredau as my co-writer.
Writing with Christoph was quite unique. At some point we started discussing theater and had the idea for a comedy in which two young men offered themselves as "male prostitutes." (This idea had come up during one of my earlier writing sessions with Christoph.) I have previously written another comedy script featuring this concept (See previous section for details.)
It was fascinating that the title for my play came to me before even writing it: "Welcome to Chez Andre". We initially considered calling the show "Chez Roger", but this may have presented some difficulties for actors performing it as it needs to be repeated often on stage. Shortly before the end, we changed Roger to Andre. Christoph hails from Lower Rhine and works as a nurse by profession; an avid film buff he makes his home into something similar to an actual cinema! While very interested in theater as an activity - though perhaps not predisposed towards this profession. Right from the beginning, he knew we must co-write this piece together - which means sitting together at a computer as we write and coming up with its plot as we type. At first it was an unfamiliar and unfamiliar writing style for me; at times there

would be suggestions from my editor that weren't something I agreed with - though sometimes vice versa. Every now and then I had to rein in his enthusiasm when his ideas went too far; but on many occasions he wrote things I never could have written myself that were brilliant and insightful. Many scenes were only enhanced through this collaboration; and we believe we should be proud of its results. At least we were both extremely satisfied with "Chez Andre", and after finishing it decided not to call it quits and are currently working on our second comedy: "Four Hands for an Udder", which should hopefully be ready by autumn 2008.

As can be seen, there are various approaches to writing music with another person. If you choose to compose the entire piece as a couple, be mindful that neither partner falls victim to working on their piece alone from time to time as this could be considered unfair to one or both partners.
Should You Prefer Writing Together or Alone? Neither one should put off doing what is best for them - I will not discourage writing together, but would like to emphasize that it works equally as well when done alone - I will definitely write my 50th work solo again this time around! Find your own way and style when approaching writing together or alone!

THE END